# Tomorrow
# Is
# Beautiful

*Books by Sarah Crossan*

The Weight of Water
Apple and Rain
One
Moonrise
Toffee

Breathe
Resist

Tomorrow Is Beautiful (ed.)

*For adult readers*
Here Is the Beehive

# Tomorrow Is Beautiful

Poems to comfort, uplift and delight

Chosen by

## SARAH CROSSAN

**BLOOMSBURY**
LONDON   OXFORD   NEW YORK   NEW DELHI   SYDNEY

BLOOMSBURY YA
Bloomsbury Publishing Plc
50 Bedford Square, London WC1B 3DP, UK
29 Earlsfort Terrace, Dublin 2, Ireland

BLOOMSBURY, BLOOMSBURY YA and the Diana logo
are trademarks of Bloomsbury Publishing Plc

First published in Great Britain in 2021 by Bloomsbury Publishing Plc

A catalogue record for this book is available from the British Library

ISBN: HB: 978-1-5266-4189-2; eBook: 978-1-5266-4190-8

2 4 6 8 10 9 7 5 3 1

Typeset by Jeni Child

Printed and bound in Great Britain by CPI Group (UK) Ltd,
Croydon CR0 4YY

To find out more about our authors and books visit
www.bloomsbury.com and sign up for our newsletters

**For Mum – who taught me to hope,
believe and forgive.
You are my best friend.
I love you so much.**

# Contents

# Introduction

This collection is a gathering together of words
that bring me joy and hope, by poets I admire
intellectually and love viscerally. Reading has
guided me through the darkest days of my life,
when I had nothing but these beautiful word-cures
to heal me. During those times I would go back to
certain lines and reread them until I changed my
mind about the world, or at least had the courage
to hold out for a new day, to see if that would
bring brighter things my way.

I have always believed poetry should serve
everyone, and as the Irish Children's Literature
Laureate from 2018 to 2020, I spearheaded a
project called We Are The Poets, which sought
to deliver poems to those who thought poetry
wasn't for them, because I know this for sure:
poetry belongs to us *all*, and we must never
let anyone make us feel otherwise. I hope this
anthology will be an extension of that project,
with the added goal of inviting readers to feel
hopeful about tomorrow.

Choosing poems from such greats as Seamus
Heaney and Anne Brontë wasn't easy, but it
was wildly exciting. And even more exciting was
choosing work from incredible contemporary poets
such as Roger Robinson and Kerrie O'Brien. I've
also had the somewhat daunting opportunity to
create and reveal new work myself. As a warning,
you will not necessarily connect to all the poems
I have selected. A person's taste in poetry is as
personal as their taste in music or food. Just
because I adore pistachios doesn't mean you
should, and that's perfectly OK. So forage for the
words in this book that fill your heart, and ignore
those that don't speak to you.

As you'll see, I have included some annotations
throughout this anthology, some of which may
inform your reading, some of which are simply
personal. You can skip them, if you wish, but they
are there to give you the sense that we are having
a conversation rather than you feeling you are
reading entirely alone. If you'd like to chat more,

I'm on social media! But remember, you do not have to understand any of these poems to engage with them; in fact the converse is true: the job of these poems is to understand you.

What you'll also notice about this collection is how much space the poems have been given, all the blank areas dotted here and there. This is so that you can read and breathe. This is so that you can, if you wish, make little notes in the spaces, or even try writing a few lines of your own poetry. 'Poetry? Me?' Yes. I mean, why not?

Finally, this book is not a bible, so use it as you wish, whether that means dog-earing the corners, accidentally getting it wet in the bath or throwing it across the room! It is yours: enjoy!

*Sarah Crossan, Hove, 2021*

Here is the tiny, powerful poem I discovered during the pandemic, which inspired me to get up in the mornings, and then to compile this entire anthology. Tomorrow will be beautiful. Yes, indeed it will!

# Hope

*Emanuel Carnevali*

Tomorrow will be beautiful
For tomorrow comes out of the lake.

Whenever something awful happens, particularly when I lose something I didn't want to lose, I feel an ugly sense of injustice. What I admire about Naomi Shahab Nye's poem is the ways in which she draws loss as a gift. Once we hit rock bottom, we will know and appreciate kindness.

# Kindness

*Naomi Shihab Nye*

Before you know what kindness really is
you must lose things,
feel the future dissolve in a moment
like salt in a weakened broth.
What you held in your hand,
what you counted and carefully saved,
all this must go so you know
how desolate the landscape can be
between the regions of kindness.
How you ride and ride
thinking the bus will never stop,
the passengers eating maize and chicken
will stare out the window forever.

Before you learn the tender gravity of kindness
you must travel where the Indian in a white poncho
lies dead by the side of the road.
You must see how this could be you,
how he too was someone
who journeyed through the night with plans
and the simple breath that kept him alive.

Before you know kindness as the deepest thing inside,
you must know sorrow as the other deepest thing.
You must wake up with sorrow.
You must speak to it till your voice
catches the thread of all sorrows
and you see the size of the cloth.
Then it is only kindness that makes sense anymore,
only kindness that ties your shoes
and sends you out into the day to gaze at bread,
only kindness that raises its head
from the crowd of the world to say
It is I you have been looking for,
and then goes with you everywhere
like a shadow or a friend.

Oswald's poem about the strength of water is also
a poem about patience. Just as the seasons take
time to turn, our hopes may require that we wait.

There's a lovely video on the Griffin Poetry Prize
YouTube channel of Alice Oswald herself reciting this
piece. Check it out, if you can, as you'll really be able
to hear the musicality of her rhyming couplets* through
her recitation.

* A 'rhyming couplet' is simply a pair of successive lines that rhyme.

# A Short Story of Falling

*Alice Oswald*

It is the story of the falling rain
to turn into a leaf and fall again

it is the secret of a summer shower
to steal the light and hide it in a flower

and every flower a tiny tributary
that from the ground flows green and momentary

is one of water's wishes and this tale
hangs in a seed-head smaller than my thumbnail

if only I a passer-by could pass
as clear as water through a plume of grass

to find the sunlight hidden at the tip
turning to seed a kind of lifting rain drip

then I might know like water how to balance
the weight of hope against the light of patience

water which is so raw so earthy-strong
and lurks in cast-iron tanks and leaks along

drawn under gravity towards my tongue
to cool and fill the pipe-work of this song

which is the story of the falling rain
that rises to the light and falls again

When your heart is broken, it's easy to believe that the best course of action is to rush out and find new love, but O'Brien advocates for emptiness. When the time is right, love will find you.

# Bud

*Kerrie O'Brien*

I think you need to be empty
To fall in love

To have been pure in yourself
For long enough
To know who you are again.

There needs to have been a winter
Where you were bare
And elegant as an orchid

Moving towards the light but in no rush
Holding your grief well

Not waiting, expecting
But quietly knowing

There will be layers of new
Flowering softness

You will tremble with life

The buds will split open
Again and again.

We tend to see the endings of things as the only thing that was - but life is about the entire journey. Icarus flew too close to the sun and fell, yes. But Icarus flew. And that is not failure.

Included for AM.

# Failing and Flying

*Jack Gilbert*

Everyone forgets that Icarus also flew.
It's the same when love comes to an end,
or the marriage fails and people say
they knew it was a mistake, that everybody
said it would never work. That she was
old enough to know better. But anything
worth doing is worth doing badly.
Like being there by that summer ocean
on the other side of the island while
love was fading out of her, the stars
burning so extravagantly those nights that
anyone could tell you they would never last.
Every morning she was asleep in my bed
like a visitation, the gentleness in her
like antelope standing in the dawn mist.
Each afternoon I watched her coming back
through the hot stony field after swimming,
the sea light behind her and the huge sky
on the other side of that. Listened to her
while we ate lunch. How can they say
the marriage failed? Like the people who

came back from Provence (when it was Provence)
and said it was pretty but the food was greasy.
I believe Icarus was not failing as he fell,
but just coming to the end of his triumph.

Although it is inevitable that we have to say goodbye to people we love, we never have to say goodbye to our memories of them. I just love this gently reassuring poem about grief.

It's important to read Anne Brontë's poem in the context of her life, which was no picnic: Anne was one of six children, but lost her mother as well as four siblings before she herself died at only twenty-nine years old.

# Farewell

*Anne Brontë*

Farewell to thee! but not farewell
To all my fondest thoughts of thee:
Within my heart they still shall dwell;
And they shall cheer and comfort me.

O, beautiful, and full of grace!
If thou hadst never met mine eye,
I had not dreamed a living face
Could fancied charms so far outvie.

If I may ne'er behold again
That form and face so dear to me,
Nor hear thy voice, still would I fain
Preserve, for aye, their memory.

That voice, the magic of whose tone
Can wake an echo in my breast,
Creating feelings that, alone,
Can make my tranced spirit blest.

That laughing eye, whose sunny beam
My memory would not cherish less; –
And oh, that smile! whose joyous gleam
Nor mortal language can express.

Adieu, but let me cherish, still,
The hope with which I cannot part.
Contempt may wound, and coldness chill,
But still it lingers in my heart.

And who can tell but Heaven, at last,
May answer all my thousand prayers,
And bid the future pay the past
With joy for anguish, smiles for tears?

Grief is the Thing with Feathers

Technically this excerpt is in prose, but I desperately wanted to include it to give you a taste of Porter's incredibly poetic novel. Here we have the ending – SPOILER ALERT! – where a father has taken his children with him to scatter their mother's ashes and say goodbye. It is so hopeful and beautiful, the characters stumbling forward with life and love, it makes me cry buckets every single time I read it.

# *from* **Grief is the Thing with Feathers**

*Max Porter*

The ashes stirred and seemed eager so I tilted the tin
and I yelled into the wind

I LOVE YOU I LOVE YOU I LOVE YOU

and up they went, the sense of a cloud, the failure of
clouds, scientifically quick and visually hopeless, a
murder of little burnt birds flecked against the grey
sky, the grey sea, the white sun, and gone. And the
boys were behind me, a tide-wall of laughter and
yelling, hugging my legs, tripping and grabbing,
leaping, spinning, stumbling, roaring, shrieking and
the boys shouted

I LOVE YOU I LOVE YOU I LOVE YOU

and their voice was the life and song of their mother.
Unfinished. Beautiful. Everything.

# until

*Sarah Crossan*

when caterwauling wakes you at 5 a.m.
and you can't get back to sleep –
wondering whether or not the stray tom has
left another mauled pigeon on your driveway –
it seems the day will be a disaster

    until the egg poaches perfectly
    and the jam spreads without tearing the toast
    and outside the rain hesitates
    long enough for you to enjoy breakfast
    on the patio
    and witness the sun rise

We discovered Naomi Rae, who wrote 'When All This Is Over' at aged eighteen, as we were compiling this anthology. This is the first time it has ever been published in print and we hope you love it.

# When All This Is Over

*Naomi Rae*

I'm going to run till the end of the beach in Aberdyfi,
Till it turns into the beach in Tywyn,
Till it turns into the Promenade,
Till it turns into the rocks leaning into the sea.
When all this is over, I won't turn back.

The damp air will drizzle in through my panting breath:
slight sharp pain each time. The immeasurable white mist
won't let me see if I could jump over the rocks.
I will untie my laces with numb sweaty fingers,
Peel off my sharp scented socks. My soles will feel
the edge of the earth's smooth firmness.
When all this is over, I'm going to jump in,
swoop down into the darkness, stretch
my arms to their full span no walls to push against,
run the gritty sea floor against my fingers,
I want a jellyfish to sting me.

Do you remember when my only fear was their sting?
You had to lift me above each new wave.
I'm not afraid of them now.

Throw me in.

There is just too much good advice in this long prose poem to pick out every gem. But the punchline is pretty cool: 'It is still a beautiful world … Strive to be happy.'

(My own copy of *Desiderata* contains the following inscription inside the cover: 'To Sarah, Wishing you years of happiness on this your 17th birthday. Love always, Mum xxx'.)

# Desiderata

*Max Ehrmann*

Go placidly amid the noise and the haste, and remember what peace there may be in silence. As far as possible, without surrender, be on good terms with all persons.

Speak your truth quietly and clearly; and listen to others, even to the dull and the ignorant; they too have their story.

Avoid loud and aggressive persons; they are vexatious to the spirit. If you compare yourself with others, you may become vain or bitter, for always there will be greater and lesser persons than yourself.

Enjoy your achievements as well as your plans. Keep interested in your own career, however humble; it is a real possession in the changing fortunes of time.

Exercise caution in your business affairs, for the world is full of trickery. But let this not blind you to what virtue there is; many persons strive for high ideals, and everywhere life is full of heroism.

Be yourself. Especially, do not feign affection. Neither be cynical about love; for in the face of all aridity and disenchantment, it is as perennial as the grass.

Take kindly the counsel of the years, gracefully surrendering the things of youth.

Nurture strength of spirit to shield you in sudden misfortune. But do not distress yourself with dark imaginings. Many fears are born of fatigue and loneliness.

Beyond a wholesome discipline, be gentle with yourself. You are a child of the universe no less than the trees and the stars; you have a right to be here.

And whether or not it is clear to you, no doubt the universe is unfolding as it should. Therefore be at peace with God, whatever you conceive Him to be. And whatever your labors and aspirations, in the noisy confusion of life, keep peace in your soul. With all its sham, drudgery and broken dreams, it is still a beautiful world. Be cheerful. Strive to be happy.

When I am lost, my instinct is to try to find a way back on to the path I was following. Wagoner suggests a different method: 'Stand still.' I guess if we want to find a way out of a forest or a painful situation, the first thing we must do is acknowledge that we are lost. And then listen to what's happening around us so we can get our bearings.

# Lost

*David Wagoner*

Stand still. The trees ahead and bushes beside you
Are not lost. Wherever you are is called Here,
And you must treat it as a powerful stranger,
Must ask permission to know it and be known.
The forest breathes. Listen. It answers,
I have made this place around you.
If you leave it, you may come back again, saying Here.
No two trees are the same to Raven.
No two branches are the same to Wren.
If what a tree or a bush does is lost on you,
You are surely lost. Stand still.* The forest knows
Where you are. You must let it find you.

* The repetition of 'Stand still', especially sitting in its own separate
sentence, makes it feel like a very direct order – which I have to
admit I always find helpful when I'm frantic.

One good thing that came out of the pandemic
was that we were all forced to slow down. Frantically
rushing from school to a music lesson to the shops
to the train station became impossible. Stopping
to appreciate the world around us became easier
because having nothing at all to do was normal!
I hope I can hold on to just a little of that quietness,
however full my days are in the future.

# Leisure

*W.H. Davies*

What is this life if, full of care,
We have no time to stand and stare?

No time to stand beneath the boughs
And stare as long as sheep or cows.

No time to see, when woods we pass,
Where squirrels hide their nuts in grass.

No time to see, in broad daylight,
Streams full of stars, like skies at night.

No time to turn at Beauty's glance,
And watch her feet, how they can dance.

No time to wait till her mouth can
Enrich that smile her eyes began.

A poor life this if, full of care,
We have no time to stand and stare.

I recently gave my daughter a YES DAY! Have you seen the movie? The gist of it is that for twenty-four hours you must say yes to whatever your child asks (unless it's illegal or dangerous). I was convinced it would be a total nightmare but agreed anyway. And do you know what? All she really wanted was for me to be present to her. She asked me to get up at 6 a.m. and go on the trampoline. She wanted to paint my face and drink hot chocolate in the garden. I mean, she also asked for Oreo waffles with sprinkles for breakfast and to play the penny slots on the pier, but overall she simply requested together-time, and it made me realise two things: I say no, when I could say yes, and I need to be more in the moment.

# More in the Moment

*Sarah Crossan*

When my daughter is asleep
I always wish I was more in the moment
instead of worrying about
the consequences of poor parenting.

So what that she wanted extra ice cream
        and to linger in the park?
              That spider frame is epic.

When my daughter is asleep
I watch her slack jaw
and twitching lips
I want to rip open my own chest
        to give her the air
        in my lungs
because she would use that oxygen
better than I ever do –
        bounding through mud in her school shoes,
        eating cake with her hands,
        inviting the wet dog on to the sofa.

When my daughter is asleep
I am full of regrets
instead of there with her
in the night
enjoying the bitterness of her warm breath.

When she wakes she says,
'Can I have some of my Easter egg?'
and I say, 'No,'
instinctively
before correcting myself.
'Why not?'

Why worry about the dentist
when it is a Saturday
and there is cold chocolate in the fridge?

This is the poem for you, if you're sure you'll never find love. Maybe you won't ... but maybe it'll find you!

If you haven't met Anaxagorou's work before, a good place to start is his 2013 album, *It Will Come to You*, with Karim Kamar. You can find it on most music streaming services.

# It Will Come to You

*Anthony Anaxagorou*

Love will come to you
I'm sure of that.

It will come to you
as you are counting the last few breaths
of your life's hope,
as the final feeling in your body
rolls itself into a long purple numbness,
as the alcohol becomes honey
and your only song sinks into stone.

It will come to you
as you sit exhausted on the lips of water
waiting to be kissed by its gorgeous suicide,
when each night feels like a war
reinventing itself in your bones
and every bit of sad news
was written by your hand.

It will come to you

just before you leave, just before you pack

your past away and leave the future

to those whose eyes own it,

when there is nothing left but damp space

nothing left but limp memories to live amongst

as the great earth stretches itself out before you

inviting you to end and die in its stillness.

It will come to you

I'm sure of that, and fly a kite on your wounds

to which you will curl the final tear

around your finger, open your arms

and hold your love, as if it were the last branch

reaching out from the side of a giant mountain

and you've been falling your whole life.

It will come to you
in the same way it left you
(unexpected)
with your shivering heart throwing itself
to the lightning

blind
    thunderous
        and mad.

William Morris was a massive over-achiever, famous
for painting and poetry, but particularly textiles.
Give him a google.

# from **Love is Enough**

*William Morris*

Love is enough: though the World be a-waning,
And the woods have no voice but the voice of complaining,
  Though the sky be too dark for dim eyes to discover
The gold-cups and daisies fair blooming thereunder,
Though the hills be held shadows, and the sea a dark wonder
  And this day draw a veil over all deeds pass'd over,
Yet their hands shall not tremble, their feet shall not falter;
The void shall not weary, the fear shall not alter
  These lips and these eyes of the loved and the lover.

If romance has failed you, this may be the poem for you.
I could footnote each brilliant line with praise, but I'll
leave it clean so you can find your own meaning.

# Epilogue

*Kei Miller*

Let us not repeat the easy lies about eternity and love.

We have fallen out of love before –

Like children surpassing the borders of their beds,

Woken by gravity, the suddenness of tiles.

So it is we have opened our eyes in the dark,

Found ourselves far from all that was safe and soft.

So it is we have nursed red bruises.

If we are amazed at anything let it be this:

Not that we have fallen from love,

But that we were always resurrected into it,

Like children who climb sweetly back into bed.

This is the title poem from a collection I have never published (or shown to anyone) called *Notes from the Pit*. I feel a bit wobbly sharing it like this, because I wrote those poems not for anyone else to read, but to keep myself going during a particularly hard period of my life.

If you do write, you're under no obligation to share your words with the world. You can write simply for yourself, to express a truth or ask a question. A lot of my writing stays hidden, and I think that's OK.

Dedicated to Zareena.

# Notes from the Pit

*Sarah Crossan*

When I start berating myself for not
paying the gas bill on time
or calling a friend who texted about her birthday dinner
or running more than two measly miles on flat ground
I think of the pit
and tell myself I am winning.

It's easy to forget that place.

My friends used to call down:
    *Are you OK?*
I wasn't, and I couldn't get out, but I'd say,
    *Yes, yes, I'm OK.*

It was dark.
My arms were noughts and crosses.
I weighed less than a greyhound.
I wished my mother had a happier daughter.
The sun set. The sun rose.

Someone kept pretending he'd help me out
but just as quick he'd turn his back on me.

My friend was like,
> *Need anything?*
I said,
> *Yeah. A rope.*
She laughed and threw down a spade.
She couldn't trust me with anything else.

I learned not to believe in rescuers.

I got digging.
Sideways at first.
Just to know my muscles worked.
The sun set. The sun rose.

I made a wide pit for myself.
I cried myself to sleep at noon
and again at bedtime.
I asked for a ladder
but no one heard me;
everyone was busy by then.

       *We have lives, you know.*
The sun set. The sun rose.


Eventually I dug enough soil to make a mountain.
I could have climbed out.
I didn't.
I started to enjoy the digging.
The pit itself.
I decorated it, so I'd feel more at home.


It wasn't like a prison.
It was better and worse than that.
I'd been thrown into it.
The sun set. The sun rose.

When I got out no one even noticed I'd been missing.
Everyone thought the weight loss suited me.
I bought an expensive coat.
I smiled like a superstar.

I didn't know how to explain what had happened.
My house was gone.
I had a new dog.
My daughter was grown up.

When I'm in bed at night telling myself how
much more I should be doing
I remember the pit.

The sun sets.

The sun rises.

But I am above ground.
I keep the spade beneath my bed just in case.

# Joy

## *Hilda Conkling*

Joy is not a thing you can see.

It is what you feel when you watch waves breaking,

Or when you peer through a net of woven violet stems

In Spring grass.

It is not sunlight, not moonlight,

But a separate shining.

Joy lives behind people's eyes.*

*\* Another poem/song that explores this idea is Kae Tempest's 'People's Faces', which you can hear on their album* The Books of Traps and Lessons *(2019).*

For a new recruit to poetry, the work of E.E. Cummings can be daunting. Even the way the poetry looks is different to what we might expect. As you can see here, Cummings enjoyed breaking grammatical rules and used the page as a painter might use a canvas, playing with punctuation and space. But the way to read Cummings is as you would read any poetry – aloud and with a booming, bogus confidence!

This is one of Cummings's best known love poems, and I tend to read it quickly, imagining the narrator struggling to find the words that will measure up to the intensity of his feelings.

# [i carry your heart with me(i carry it in]

*E.E. Cummings*

i carry your heart with me(i carry it in
my heart)i am never without it(anywhere
i go you go,my dear;and whatever is done
by only me is your doing,my darling)
                                             i fear
no fate(for you are my fate,my sweet)i want
no world(for beautiful you are my world,my true)
and it's you are whatever a moon has always meant
and whatever a sun will always sing is you

here is the deepest secret nobody knows
(here is the root of the root and the bud of the bud
and the sky of the sky of a tree called life;which grows
higher than soul can hope or mind can hide)
and this is the wonder that's keeping the stars apart

i carry your heart(i carry it in my heart)

Anaxagorou's promise of love, as a sort of compensation for all you have endured, may seem a bit of a stretch. But surely this is why we continue to walk over coals day after day. Something 'you will come to call love' is heading your way.

# For All You've Endured

*Anthony Anaxagorou*

it will make you mad
to the point you find yourself biting down
on your own blood

it will let you down
lowering you into its nettled bitterness
and you'll find yourself bloated with worry
(sleepless)

skin littered with the graffiti of your marking past
which you will come to call life
and you will come to call hard

up until the moment it eases
like the hearing of good news
and says for all your troubles

for all you've endured
I will give you to keep
what you will come to call love

# Why Bother, Mother?

*Sarah Crossan*

I ask my mother
why bother when there's always someone
getting sacked,
getting dumped,
getting cancer,
ordering funeral flowers,
crying in an airport,
crying in a toilet,
crying on a train,
cutting their arms,
cutting their losses,
hoping for a baby,
hoping for a bleed,
eating from a foodbank,
refusing to eat,
unable to sleep,
unable to breathe,
broken boned
broken hearted,
broken?

She says, to love.

To be loved.

Just once.

'The Great Lover' is a poem I come back to again and again. This is an excerpt from the original, but it's my favourite part, where Brooke basically lists all the things he loves. When I was a teacher, I'd show students this stanza and ask them to imitate it. What simple pleasures make you smile? What sensations delight you? Thinking in this way gets us focused on life's quiet moments and is a reminder that pleasures are always close at hand. Start with a bakery window if you're stuck for ideas!

Rupert Brooke was gorgeous – he could have been an elf in *Lord of the Rings*. You should google him so you can see his face. Sadly he died in 1915 at only twenty-seven years old.

# from **The Great Lover**

*Rupert Brooke*

These I have loved:
    White plates and cups, clean-gleaming,
Ringed with blue lines; and feathery, faery dust;
Wet roofs, beneath the lamp-light; the strong crust
Of friendly bread; and many-tasting food;
Rainbows; and the blue bitter smoke of wood;
And radiant raindrops couching in cool flowers;
And flowers themselves, that sway through sunny hours,
Dreaming of moths that drink them under the moon;
Then, the cool kindliness of sheets, that soon
Smooth away trouble; and the rough male kiss
Of blankets; grainy wood; live hair that is
Shining and free; blue-massing clouds; the keen
Unpassioned beauty of a great machine;
The benison of hot water; furs to touch;
The good smell of old clothes; and other such –
The comfortable smell of friendly fingers,
Hair's fragrance, and the musty reek that lingers
About dead leaves and last year's ferns ...

Dear Rupert,
Forgive me.
Sarah

# These I Have Loved

*Sarah Crossan*

These I have loved:
                    Wide trees, centuries toughened,
stubbornly ascending into the sky;
the delicate diving of butterflies;
smoking red-brick chimneys; peonies;
the willowy sigh of sleeping children; cheese;
crisp, clean notebooks; gentle strolling by the sea;
unexpected packages; tea with honey;
a biro at the bottom of a tote;
fizzy water with lime; casting my vote;
achy stiff and sore from running hills; lipstick;
stormy cliff tops; real glass at a picnic;
pairs of magpies and their glossy treasures;
organic red wine in generous measures;
My daughter's smile and rage and smell ...
                    These I have loved.

This poem could be a scene in a horror film, but the speaker flips what could be frightening into a blessing.

# The Wasps

*David Constantine*

The apples on the tree are full of wasps.
Red apples, racing like hearts. The summer pushes
Her tongue into the winter's throat.

But at six today, like rain, the first drops,
The wasps came battering softly at the black glass.
They want the light, the cold is at their backs.

That morning last year when the lamp had been left on
The strange room terrified the heart in me,
I could not place myself, didn't know my own

Insect scribble: then saw the whole soft
Pelt of wasps, its underbelly, the long black pane
Yellow with visitants, it seethed, the glass sounded.

I bless my life: that so much wants in.

Charlotte Brontë is best known for her novel *Jane Eyre*, but she began her writing career as a poet. And here she encourages the reader to have courage in the face of grief when Death 'calls our best away'. I really like how she describes hope, which is 'Unconquered' in us, having 'golden wings / Still strong to bear us well'.

# Life

*Charlotte Brontë*

Life, believe, is not a dream
    So dark as sages say;
Oft a little morning rain
    Foretells a pleasant day.
Sometimes there are clouds of gloom,
    But these are transient all;
If the shower will make the roses bloom,
    Oh, why lament its fall?
    Rapidly, merrily,
Life's sunny hours flit by,
    Gratefully, cheerily,
Enjoy them as they fly!

What though Death at times steps in,
        And calls our best away?
What though sorrow seems to win,
        O'er hope, a heavy sway?
Yet Hope again elastic springs,
        Unconquered, though she fell;
Still buoyant are her golden wings,
        Still strong to bear us well.
            Manfully, fearlessly,
        The day of trial bear,
            For gloriously, victoriously,
        Can courage quell despair!

Roger Robinson's collection *A Portable Paradise* is not always easy reading, but this, the final poem, left me so uplifted, that when I turned the final page I immediately went back to the beginning so I could experience the book all over again.

# A Portable Paradise

*Roger Robinson*

And if I speak of Paradise,
then I'm speaking of my grandmother
who told me to carry it always
on my person, concealed, so
no one else would know but me.
That way they can't steal it, she'd say.
And if life puts you under pressure,
trace its ridges in your pocket,
smell its piney scent on your handkerchief,
hum its anthem under your breath.
And if your stresses are sustained and daily,
get yourself to an empty room - be it hotel,
hostel or hovel - find a lamp
and empty your paradise onto a desk:
your white sands, green hills and fresh fish.
Shine the lamp on it like the fresh hope
of morning, and keep staring at it till you sleep.

One of the things I'm always banging on about is the joy of learning poems by heart. If you try this, you'll learn the poem with your body as well as your brain, and anything about the language that feels confusing just falls away after constant repetition. If you're new to memorisation, start with something short that has a regular rhyme scheme, like this joyful poem by Rossetti. It's just four lines. Give it a go! If you prefer something more modern, just find something you love and learn a section of it. I know huge of chunks of Shakespeare, and I have to say that it also serves as a very good party piece!

# Fly Away, Fly Away

*Christina Rossetti*

Fly away, fly away over the sea,
Sun-loving swallow, for summer is done;
Come again, come again, come back to me,
Bringing the summer and bringing the sun.

The repetition in this poem is just gorgeous!

# A Navajo Prayer

*Anon.*

In beauty may I walk

All day long may I walk

Through the returning seasons may I walk

Beautifully will I possess again

Beautifully birds,

Beautifully joyful birds

On the trail marked with pollen may I walk

With grasshoppers about my feet may I walk

With dew about my feet may I walk

With beauty may I walk

With beauty before me may I walk

With beauty behind me may I walk

With beauty above me may I walk

With beauty all around me may I walk

In old age, wandering on a trail of beauty, lively, may I walk

In old age, wandering on a trail of beauty, living again, may I walk

It is finished in beauty.

It is finished in beauty.

A friend recently messaged me to say she was feeling something strange and unsettling. She believed, but couldn't be sure, that she was ... happy? I told her not to worry, that it would soon pass and she'd feel like her old self again soon. Because that's the sort of friend I am!

Included for NS.

# So Much Happiness

*Naomi Shihab Nye*

It is difficult to know what to do with so much happiness.
With sadness there is something to rub against,
a wound to tend with lotion and cloth.
When the world falls in around you, you have pieces to pick up,
something to hold in your hands, like ticket stubs or change.

But happiness floats.
It doesn't need you to hold it down.
It doesn't need anything.
Happiness lands on the roof of the next house, singing,
and disappears when it wants to.
You are happy either way.
Even the fact that you once lived in a peaceful tree house
and now live over a quarry of noise and dust
cannot make you unhappy.
Everything has a life of its own,
it too could wake up filled with possibilities
of coffee cake and ripe peaches,
and love even the floor which needs to be swept,
the soiled linens and scratched records ...

Since there is no place large enough
to contain so much happiness,
you shrug, you raise your hands, and it flows out of you
into everything you touch. You are not responsible.
You take no credit, as the night sky takes no credit
for the moon, but continues to hold it, and share it,
and in that way, be known.

Walt Whitman is sometimes called the father of free verse (though he didn't actually invent it) and is my hero. Free verse is when a poem doesn't follow a particular pattern and often mimics speech. This is how I write my verse novels, so I'm very grateful to him for turning this practice into something seen as worthwhile! He does use plenty of other poetic devices in his poems, though, the most obvious here being repetition ('O me! O life!') and alliteration ('faithless ... fill'd ... foolish').

# O Me! O Life!

*Walt Whitman*

O me! O life! of the questions of these recurring,

Of the endless trains of the faithless, of cities fill'd with the foolish,

Of myself forever reproaching myself, (for who more foolish than I, and who more faithless?)

Of eyes that vainly crave the light, of the objects mean, of the struggle ever renew'd,

Of the poor results of all, of the plodding and sordid crowds I see around me,

Of the empty and useless years of the rest, with the rest me intertwined,

The question, O me! so sad, recurring – What good amid these, O me, O life?

*Answer.**

That you are here – that life exists and identity,

That the powerful play goes on, and you may contribute a verse.

* I love how Whitman actually gives us an answer to the meaning of life: make a contribution to this world!

This is an excerpt from my first novel for adults. It is about taking risks, which we do every day anyway, even by choosing to get out of bed!

# from **Here is the Beehive**

*Sarah Crossan*

How can we know which days
will be the turning points?

So long as we live,
we gamble.

Red.
Black.

Put it all on Number 11.

'Rest if you must, but don't you quit.'

# Don't Quit

*Edgar A. Guest*

When things go wrong, as they sometimes will,
When the road you're trudging seems all uphill,
When the funds are low and the debts are high,
And you want to smile but you have to sigh,
When care is pressing you down a bit –
Rest if you must, but don't you quit.

Life is queer with its twists and turns.
As every one of us sometimes learns,
And many a failure turns about
When he might have won had he stuck it out.
Don't give up though the pace seems slow –
You may succeed with another blow.

Often the goal is nearer than
It seems to a faint and faltering man,
Often the struggler has given up
When he might have captured the victor's cup,
And he learned too late when the night came down
How close he was to the golden crown.

Success is failure turned inside out,

The silver tint of the clouds of doubt,

And you never can tell how close you are,

It may be near when it seems afar,

So stick to the fight when you're hardest hit –

It's when things seem worst that you must not quit.

This very well-known poem by literary giant Langston Hughes is a good example of what is known as an 'extended metaphor', where the writer exploits a single idea, drawing multiple parallels between one thing and another.

# Mother to Son

*Langston Hughes*

Well, son, I'll tell you:
Life for me ain't been no crystal stair.
It's had tacks in it,
And splinters,
And boards torn up,
And places with no carpet on the floor—
Bare.
But all the time
I'se been a-climbin' on,
And reachin' landin's,
And turnin' corners,
And sometimes goin' in the dark
Where there ain't been no light.
So, boy, don't you turn back.
Don't you set down on the steps
'Cause you finds it's kinder hard.
Don't you fall now—
For I'se still goin', honey,
I'se still climbin',
And life for me ain't been no crystal stair.

Don't be intimidated by the Latin title of this poem, which just means 'undefeated'. Give it a read and you'll be rewarded by the final line, one of my favourites ever.

# Invictus

*William Ernest Henley*


Out of the night that covers me,
   Black as the pit from pole to pole,
I thank whatever gods may be
   For my unconquerable soul.

In the fell clutch of circumstance
   I have not winced nor cried aloud.
Under the bludgeonings of chance
   My head is bloody, but unbowed.

Beyond this place of wrath and tears
   Looms but the Horror of the shade,
And yet the menace of the years
   Finds and shall find me unafraid.

It matters not how strait the gate,
   How charged with punishments the scroll,
I am the master of my fate,
   I am the captain of my soul.

Robert Frost received four Pulitzer Prizes for Poetry in his lifetime. This is equivalent to an Oscar, a Nobel Prize, and winning *MasterChef*!

# Riders

*Robert Frost*

The surest thing there is is we are riders,
And though none too successful at it, guiders,
Through everything presented, land and tide
And now the very air, of what we ride.

What is this talked-of mystery of birth
But being mounted bareback on the earth?
We can just see the infant up astride,
His small fist buried in the bushy hide.

There is our wildest mount – a headless horse.
But though it runs unbridled off its course,
And all our blandishments would seem defied,
We have ideas yet that we haven't tried.

This is a very well-known, but also quite a slippery poem, as it can be read in a couple of ways. Many interpret the final stanza as a call to follow your own path or destiny, but many other critics have suggested it is simply a reminder that whichever path you take, there is another you missed out on, and so we are bound to regret our choices as we can never see where the alternative would have taken us.

# The Road Not Taken

*Robert Frost*

Two roads diverged in a yellow wood,
And sorry I could not travel both
And be one traveler, long I stood
And looked down one as far as I could
To where it bent in the undergrowth;

Then took the other, as just as fair,
And having perhaps the better claim,
Because it was grassy and wanted wear;
Though as for that the passing there
Had worn them really about the same,

And both that morning equally lay
In leaves no step had trodden black.
Oh, I kept the first for another day!
Yet knowing how way leads on to way,
I doubted if I should ever come back.

I shall be telling this with a sigh

Somewhere ages and ages hence:

Two roads diverged in a wood, and I –

I took the one less traveled by,

And that has made all the difference.

When people doubt you, 'just buckle in with a bit of a grin' and 'go to it'!

# It Couldn't Be Done

*Edgar A. Guest*

Somebody said that it couldn't be done
    But he with a chuckle replied
That 'maybe it couldn't', but he would be one
    Who wouldn't say so till he'd tried.
So he buckled right in with the trace of a grin
    On his face. If he worried he hid it.
He started to sing as he tackled the thing
    That couldn't be done, and he did it!

Somebody scoffed: 'Oh, you'll never do that;
    At least no one ever has done it';
But he took off his coat and he took off his hat
    And the first thing we knew he'd begun it.
With a lift of his chin and a bit of a grin,
    Without any doubting or quiddit,
He started to sing as he tackled the thing
    That couldn't be done, and he did it.

There are thousands to tell you it cannot be done,

There are thousands to prophesy failure,

There are thousands to point out to you one by one,

The dangers that wait to assail you.

But just buckle in with a bit of a grin,

Just take off your coat and go to it;

Just start in to sing as you tackle the thing

That 'cannot be done', and you'll do it.

This is one of my favourite poems in the collection.
I hope you love it as much as I do.

# Go to the Limits of Your Longing

*Rainer Maria Rilke*

God speaks to each of us as he makes us,
then walks with us silently out of the night.

These are the words we dimly hear:

You, sent out beyond your recall,
go to the limits of your longing.*
Embody me.

Flare up like a flame
and make big shadows I can move in.

Let everything happen to you: beauty and terror.
Just keep going. No feeling is final.♥
Don't let yourself lose me.

Nearby is the country they call life.
You will know it by its seriousness.

Give me your hand.

* I don't have any tattoos, but if I did, this is the line I'd have inked up my arm.
♥ And this is the quote I need to chant whenever I'm under the duvet, sobbing and hating life.

# Let No One Steal Your Dreams

*Paul Cookson*

Let no one steal your dreams
Let no one tear apart
The burning of ambition
That fires the drive inside your heart

Let no one steal your dreams
Let no one tell you that you can't
Let no one hold you back
Let no one tell you that you won't

Set your sights and keep them fixed
Set your sights on high
Let no one steal your dreams
Your only limit is the sky

Let no one steal your dreams
Follow your heart
Follow your soul
For only when you follow them
Will you feel truly whole

Set your sights and keep them fixed

Set your sights on high

Let no one steal your dreams

Your only limit is the sky

For years I had Henry Ford's famous quote on my kitchen wall: 'Whether you think you can or think you can't – you're right.' And I believe this – that our beliefs about our capabilities determine our outcomes. 'You've got to think high to rise.'

# Thinking

*Walter D. Wintle*

If you think you are beaten, you are;
If you think you dare not, you don't.
If you'd like to win, but you think you can't,
It is almost a cinch you won't.

If you think you'll lose, you've lost;
For out in this world we find
Success begins with a fellow's will
It's all in the state of mind.

If you think you're outclassed, you are;
You've got to think high to rise.
You've got to be sure of yourself before
You can ever win the prize.

Life's battles don't always go
To the stronger or faster man;
But sooner or later the person who wins
Is the one who thinks he can!

Audre Lorde was an American writer and civil rights activist. Her poems address issues of feminism, lesbianism, and the exploration of black identity, most especially black female identity. This poem seems to speak to, and offer a gentle power back to, all marginalised people who 'were never meant to survive'.

# A Litany for Survival

*Audre Lorde*

For those of us who live at the shoreline
standing upon the constant edges of decision
crucial and alone
for those of us who cannot indulge
the passing dreams of choice
who love in doorways coming and going
in the hours between dawns
looking inward and outward
at once before and after
seeking a now that can breed
futures
like bread in our children's mouths
so their dreams will not reflect
the death of ours;

For those of us
who were imprinted with fear
like a faint line in the center of our foreheads
learning to be afraid with our mother's milk
for by this weapon
this illusion of some safety to be found
the heavy-footed hoped to silence us
For all of us
this instant and this triumph
We were never meant to survive.

And when the sun rises we are afraid
it might not remain
when the sun sets we are afraid
it might not rise in the morning
when our stomachs are full we are afraid
of indigestion
when our stomachs are empty we are afraid
we may never eat again
when we are loved we are afraid
love will vanish

when we are alone we are afraid
love will never return
and when we speak we are afraid
our words will not be heard
nor welcomed
but when we are silent
we are still afraid

So it is better to speak
remembering
we were never meant to survive.

As you'll have noticed, this collection is not divided into chapters. If it were, however, *Ode to Maya Angelou* would need its own distinct space, as I can't help but think that most of the poets who have written on the theme of 'rising', including those below, are responding to 'Still I Rise', one of Angelou's most popular poems. The poem itself has become something of an anthem for empowerment and a declaration of the dignity of victims of injustice, especially those within African American communities. Maya Angelou was both a writer and a fierce political activist. She was awarded the Presidential Medal of Freedom in 2011 by Barak Obama.

# Still I Rise

*Maya Angelou*

You may write me down in history
With your bitter, twisted lies,
You may trod me in the very dirt
But still, like dust, I'll rise.

Does my sassiness upset you?
Why are you beset with gloom?
'Cause I walk like I've got oil wells
Pumping in my living room.

Just like moons and like suns,
With the certainty of tides,
Just like hopes springing high,
Still I'll rise.

Did you want to see me broken?
Bowed head and lowered eyes?
Shoulders falling down like teardrops,
Weakened by my soulful cries?

Does my haughtiness offend you?
Don't you take it awful hard
'Cause I laugh like I've got gold mines
Diggin' in my own backyard.

You may shoot me with your words,
You may cut me with your eyes,
You may kill me with your hatefulness,
But still, like air, I'll rise.

Does my sexiness upset you?
Does it come as a surprise
That I dance like I've got diamonds
At the meeting of my thighs?

Out of the huts of history's shame
I rise
Up from a past that's rooted in pain
I rise
I'm a black ocean, leaping and wide,
Welling and swelling I bear in the tide.

Leaving behind nights of terror and fear

I rise

Into a daybreak that's wondrously clear

I rise

Bringing the gifts that my ancestors gave,

I am the dream and the hope of the slave.

I rise

I rise

I rise.

# Majestic

*Kwame Alexander*

*for Maya Angelou*

Rise
into the wonder
of daybreak.

Be a rainbow in the cloud.
Be a free bird on the back of the night wind.
Shine on, honey!

Walk with joy in your golden feet
over crystal seas
and purpled mountains.

Know your beauty
is a thunder
your precious heart unsalable.

Be brave,
like a new seed bursting
with extraordinary promise.

Shine on, honey!
Know you
are phenomenal.

# Rise

*Jay Hulme*

Rise, Child,
and take your place in these stars,
they made themselves bold for your eyes.
You may not know your future, Child,
but rise.

All awaits you here,
broken into the fragments of light
that glitter so softly
in the darkened skies,
you were born,
and so may rise.

The air you breathe
was exhaled by Achilles
so long ago
that we have fixed the flaws
that failed him.

Now you are burdened
with nothing more
than the endless possibility
of this soaring sky
that stretches out so far
we call it infinite.

Within it you may make your home
like a God, or an eagle
that never dies.
Look to the stars,
Child, rise.

# Rise

*Abigail Cook*

And when they try
to clip your wings,
tell you
to sit down, shut up:
rise.

When they tell you
you are too much this way
and too little that way:
rise.

Remember you are falcon bones
and phoenix wings,
so fly.

You are worthy.

# Rise

*Sarah Crossan*

Even as it falls apart,
as the ending you never considered possible
blindsides your joy,
rise.

Even as everything turns to cinder,
and no one is prepared to promise
it will feel OK again,
rise.

Even as darkness shovels in more shit
than you ever imagined one person
could contend with,
rise.

Even as you realise an ellipsis would be a lie
...
try to rise.

Rise to the maybe of dawn.

Rise as it all falls apart.

I have twice seen Kae Tempest perform live, and each time I left feeling entirely understood, as well as part of something much bigger than myself. It was difficult to choose a piece of their work to include, but I have chosen this poem from *The Book of Traps and Lessons*, as that repeated line, 'Hold your own', feels like such an important mantra. It's easy to be unnerved by the will of others, or feel shame about who we are. But accepting everything about ourselves, all the pain and the joy, needn't scare us. We can turn everything that is true into a source of power.

# Hold Your Own

*Kae Tempest*

But, when time pulls lives apart

Hold your own

When everything is fluid, nothing can be known with any
   certainty

Hold your own

Hold it till you feel it there

As dark and dense and wet as earth

As vast and bright and sweet as air

When all there is, is knowing that you feel what you are
   feeling

Hold your own

Ask your hands to know the things they hold

I know, the days are reeling past in such squealing blasts

But stop for breath and you will know it's yours

Swaying like an open door when storms are coming

Hold

Time is an onslaught, love is a mission

We work for vocations until, in remission

We wish we'd had patience and given more time to our
   children

Feel each decision that you make

Make it, hold it

Hold your own

Hold your lovers

Hold their hands

Hold their breasts in your hands like your hands were their
  bra

Hold their face in your palms like a prayer

Hold them all night, feel them hold back

Don't hold back

Hold your own

Every pain

Every grievance

Every stab of shame

Every day spent with a demon in your brain giving chase

Hold it

Know the wolves that hunt you

In time, they will be the dogs that bring your slippers

Love them right and you will feel them kiss you when they
  come to bite

Hot snouts digging out your cuddles with their bloody
   muzzles
Hold
Nothing you can buy will ever make you more whole
This whole thing thrives on us feeling always incomplete
And it is why we will search for happiness in whatever
   thing it is we crave in the moment
And it is why we can never really find it there
It is why you will sit there with the lover that you fought for
In the car you sweated years to buy
Wearing the ring you dreamed of all your life
And some part of you will still be unsure that this is what
   you really want
Stop craving
Hold your own
But if you're satisfied with where you're at, with who you are
You won't need to buy new make-up or new outfits or new
   pots and pans
To cook new exciting recipes for new exciting people
To make yourself feel like the new exciting person you think
   you're supposed to be

Happiness, the brand, is not happiness

We are smarter than they think we are

They take us all for idiots, but that's their problem

When we behave like idiots, it becomes our problem

So, hold your own

Breathe deep on a freezing beach

Taste the salt of friendship

Notice the movement of a stranger

Hold your own

And let it be

Catching

The perfect poem to follow 'Hold Your Own'.

# A Center

*Ha Jin*

You must hold your quiet center,
where you do what only you can do.
If others call you a maniac or a fool,
just let them wag their tongues.
If some praise your perseverance,
don't feel too happy about it –
only solitude is a lasting friend.

You must hold your distant center.
Don't move even if earth and heaven quake.
If others think you are insignificant,
that's because you haven't held on long enough.
As long as you stay put year after year,
eventually you will find a world
beginning to revolve around you.*

* When someone asks if you think the world revolves around you,
  you can say, 'Not yet, but that's the goal!'

When my daughter goes into school every day I say, 'Be good. And if you can't be good ...' To which she replies, '... don't get caught!' Being 'good' is so overrated, and it's how we are conditioned to behave. How about we focus less on self-sacrifice and more on allowing ourselves to love what we love, as Oliver suggests?

# Wild Geese

*Mary Oliver*

You do not have to be good.
You do not have to walk on your knees
for a hundred miles through the desert repenting.
You only have to let the soft animal of your body
love what it loves.
Tell me about despair, yours, and I will tell you mine.
Meanwhile the world goes on.
Meanwhile the sun and the clear pebbles of the rain
are moving across the landscapes,
over the prairies and the deep trees,
the mountains and the rivers.
Meanwhile the wild geese, high in the clean blue air,
are heading home again.
Whoever you are, no matter how lonely,
the world offers itself to your imagination,
calls to you like the wild geese, harsh and exciting –
over and over announcing your place
In the family of things.

My mum loves books but never had the chance to study them when she was young, so she decided to do an A-level English course when she was in her forties. *Hamlet* was on the syllabus. She got totally stuck into her studies and booked tickets for us to see Ralph Fiennes playing the lead in *Hamlet* at the Almeida Theatre. I was a teenager, and wasn't convinced by Shakespeare, finding him pointlessly difficult. But that performance changed everything. The text was so alive and exciting on the stage. Things changed for my mum too. She became a proper nerd and passed her A-level English with flying colours. I tell you this because it really is never too late to get into poetry. And even though Shakespeare can seem stuffy at times, good directors will always make the plays feel modern and relevant. Sexy too, if you're lucky ... though not when your mum's sitting next to you, obviously.

# from **Hamlet**

*William Shakespeare*

This above all: to thine own self be true,
And it must follow, as the night the day,
Thou canst not then be false to any man.

A poem for all the over-achievers out there!

# you are enough

*Sarah Crossan*

you are enough:
you do not need to be funny
or glamorous
or bring a bottle to the party.

you are enough:
you do not need to dye your hair
or put fillers in your face
or reorder your image.

you are enough:
you do not need to work until midnight
or keep a clean house
or remember to put out the bins.

you are enough:
you do not need to read the bestseller
or watch the blockbuster
or recognise the meme.

you are enough:
you do not need to be patient
or kind
or offer up your life as a sacrifice.

you are enough:
your presence,
owning its space in the universe.

That is enough.

Hafiz was a Persian poet who was writing about 700 years ago. Those last four lines are particularly inspiring: if we could only know the light our souls emit, we would never feel alone.

# My Brilliant Image

*Hafiz*

One day the sun admitted
I am just a shadow.
I wish I could show you
The infinite incandescence
That has cast my brilliant image!

I wish I could show you,
When you are lonely or in darkness,
The Astonishing Light
Of your own Being!

Read this poem twice: the first time, read it all the way through exactly as it's written; the second time, ignore the words in brackets.

# Love

*Victoria Adukwei Bulley*


Your heart beating
      (without permission)

Your lungs breathing like clockwork
(without ever having been asked)

Your body working
      (without a thought –
without ever having demanded love
        back from you)

I was introduced to this poem by Pádraig Ó Tuama when he guided me through it on the podcast *Poetry Unbound*. I recommend you listen to that episode (30 November 2020), which unravels this poem and explains, amongst other things, that the speaker here is not arrogantly forgiving someone else but learning to forgive herself – a noble and challenging endeavour.

*Poetry Unbound* focuses on a single poem each episode, and breaks down the meaning in a way that feels refreshingly non-threatening and wise. Do check it out.

# PHASE ONE

*Dilruba Ahmed*

For leaving the fridge open
last night, I forgive you.
For conjuring white curtains
instead of living your life.

For the seedlings that wilt, now,
in tiny pots, I forgive you.
For saying *no* first
but *yes* as an afterthought.

I forgive you for hideous visions
after childbirth, brought on by loss
of sleep. And when the baby woke
repeatedly, for your silent rebuke

in the dark, 'What's your beef?'
I forgive your letting vines
overtake the garden. For fearing
your own propensity to love.

For losing, again, your bag
en route from San Francisco;
for the equally heedless drive back
on the caffeine-fueled return.

I forgive you for leaving
windows open in rain
and soaking library books
again.  For putting forth

only revisions of yourself,
with punctuation worked over,
instead of the disordered truth,
I forgive you.  For singing mostly

when the shower drowns
your voice.  For so admiring
the drummer you failed to hear
the drum. In forgotten tin cans,

may forgiveness gather.  Pooling
in gutters.  Gushing from pipes.
A great steady rain of olives
from branches, relieved

of cruelty and petty meanness.
With it, a flurry of wings, thirteen
gray pigeons.  Ointment reserved
for healers and prophets.  I forgive you.

I forgive you.  For feeling awkward
and nervous without reason.
For bearing Keats' empty vessel
with such calm you worried

you had, perhaps, no moral
center at all.  For treating your mother
with contempt when she deserved
compassion.  I forgive you.  I forgive

you.  I forgive you.  For growing
a capacity for love that is great
but matched only, perhaps,
by your loneliness.  For being unable

to forgive yourself first so you
could then forgive others and
at last find a way to become
the love that you want in this world.

Yrsa Daley-Ward is a writer who speaks to a new generation of readers and has a huge following on Instagram, where she regularly posts poems. Her work is accessible and raw. Here's a taste of her poetry, in two extracts from *Bone*, a collection I can highly recommend.

# from **things it can take twenty years and a bad liver to work out**

*Yrsa Daley-Ward*

There are parts of you
that want the sadness.
Find them out. Ask them why.

# untitled 2

*Yrsa Daley-Ward*

Seize that loveliness.
It has always been yours.

When a relationship ends, especially one for which we have sacrificed much of ourselves (and therefore become a 'stranger' to ourselves), it can be difficult to recover. In this popular poem, written in 1976, Walcott reassures us that the time will come when we will give again to ourselves and love the person we see in the mirror.

# Love After Love

*Derek Walcott*

The time will come
when, with elation
you will greet yourself arriving
at your own door, in your own mirror
and each will smile at the other's welcome,

and say, sit here. Eat.
You will love again the stranger who was your self.
Give wine. Give bread. Give back your heart
to itself, to the stranger who has loved you

all your life, whom you ignored
for another, who knows you by heart.
Take down the love letters from the bookshelf,

the photographs, the desperate notes,
peel your own image from the mirror.
Sit. Feast on your life.

The following two poems are about taking risk, opening doors, and being excited by the challenge of what is new. They will appeal to some readers but perhaps not to others: plenty of people live with a fear of scarcity, and take very few risks for fear of losing something stable. I wonder who has the happier life – the risk taker or the person who plays it safe? I have no answer!

# The Door

*Miroslav Holub*

Go and open the door.
Maybe outside there's
a tree, or a wood,
a garden,
or a magic city.

Go and open the door.
Maybe a dog's rummaging.
Maybe you'll see a face,
or an eye,
or the picture
of a picture.

Go and open the door.
If there's a fog
it will clear.

Go and open the door.
Even if there's only
the darkness ticking,
even if there's only
the hollow wind,
even if
nothing
is there,
go and open the door.

At least
there'll be
a draught.

# What If This Road

*Sheenagh Pugh*


What if this road, that has held no surprises

these many years, decided not to go

home after all; what if it could turn

left or right with no more ado

than a kite-tail? What if its tarry skin

were like a long, supple bolt of cloth,

that is shaken and rolled out, and takes

a new shape from the contours beneath?

And if it chose to lay itself down

in a new way; around a blind corner,

across hills you must climb without knowing

what's on the other side; who would not hanker

to be going, at all risks? Who wants to know

a story's end, or where a road will go?

Don't dwell on the past – it's done. Today is a new day.
'Begin again.'

# New Every Morning

*Susan Coolidge*

Every morn is the world made new.
You who are weary of sorrow and sinning,
Here is a beautiful hope for you, –
A hope for me and a hope for you.

All the past things are past and over;
The tasks are done and the tears are shed.
Yesterday's errors let yesterday cover;
Yesterday's wounds, which smarted and bled,
Are healed with the healing which night has shed.

Yesterday now is a part of forever,
Bound up in a sheaf, which God holds tight,
With glad days, and sad days, and bad days,
   which never
Shall visit us more with their bloom and their blight,
Their fulness of sunshine or sorrowful night.

Let them go, since we cannot re-live them,
Cannot undo and cannot atone;
God in his mercy receive, forgive them!
Only the new days are our own;
To-day is ours, and to-day alone.

Here are the skies all burnished brightly,
Here is the spent earth all re-born,
Here are the tired limbs springing lightly
To face the sun and to share with the morn
In the chrism of dew and the cool of dawn.

Every day is a fresh beginning;
Listen, my soul, to the glad refrain,
And, spite of old sorrow and older sinning,
And puzzles forecasted and possible pain,
Take heart with the day, and begin again.

Kennelly is an award-winning Irish poet and former university professor who worked very hard not only to produce a large body of work himself, but to demystify poetry for his students. He is not an artist who appears to take himself too seriously, but that doesn't mean we shouldn't take his work seriously.

If you'd like to see Brendan Kennelly in action, both Poetry Ireland and Bloodaxe Books have wonderful videos of him talking about and reciting his own work on their YouTube channels.

# Begin

*Brendan Kennelly*

Begin again to the summoning birds
to the sight of the light at the window,
begin to the roar of morning traffic
all along Pembroke Road.
Every beginning is a promise
born in light and dying in dark
determination and exaltation of springtime
flowering the way to work.
Begin to the pageant of queuing girls
the arrogant loneliness of swans in the canal
bridges linking the past and future
old friends passing though with us still.
Begin to the loneliness that cannot end
since it perhaps is what makes us begin,
begin to wonder at unknown faces
at crying birds in the sudden rain
at branches stark in the willing sunlight
at seagulls foraging for bread
at couples sharing a sunny secret
alone together while making good.

Though we live in a world that dreams of ending
that always seems about to give in
something that will not acknowledge conclusion
insists that we forever begin.

A poem about the importance of enjoying life's journey, and not focusing on our arrival in any particular place.

# The Door

*Andrew Wynn Owen*

Distracting rays were shining round my door
And so I stood
And stepped across the landing floor
To see if any light-source could
Be ascertained but, once I was outside,
I checked my stride.

Out there I found a stretching corridor,
So down I walked.
I had not noticed it before.
On every lintel, names were chalked
And soon I stalled at one that was well-known:
It was my own.

The hinges creaked. I cautiously went in,
Enjoying there
A room where sunlight lapped my skin
And central was a swivel chair.
It spun about. I felt a smile extend:
'Good morning, friend.'

This figure gestured me towards an arch
Marked 'Happiness'
And I, determined, moved to march
Its way, but paused: 'I should express
Some thanks—' my friend, however, waved and said,
'You go ahead.'

Once I had ventured in I felt betrayed,
As I discerned
A maze of winding walls that made
Me dizzy, sad,* until I turned
One corner and (in hope of what?) I saw
Another door.

* How often have you walked a particular path in life believing
  happiness was at the end of it, only to discover yet more
  complications ahead? It's like those very fancy all-you-can eat
  breakfast buffets, with pancake stations and fresh omelettes,
  that seem to offer endless nourishment but leave you feeling
  like a gluttonous beast by 9.45 a.m.

Eager, I entered, to a gallery
Closely comprised
Of portals, each a vacancy
For liberty. I realised
I'd never loved a room. It is the door
That I adore.

At moments of crisis, I always believe that the change
I am going through will define me, but it turns out very
few moments in life have that power. Life is complicated
and messy and long.

DISCLAIMER! only some of this poem is true.

# Things You Put Into Your Mother's Garage And Try To Forget

*Sarah Crossan*

I picked him up from the airport

and twenty minutes later,

in a McDonald's drive-thru

told him we were done.

He didn't believe me

because I had always been devoted.

I drove him to his college

and decided

when he shut the door

not to call him ever again.

I knew he'd been seeing someone.

I knew he fancied Sophie-Anna.

I found a letter he wrote to her in French.

I hated all the tennis they played together.

He called my mum

and begged her to talk sense into me.

His car had been stored in her garage

for over a year.

She told him to pick up the car and leave me alone

because I knew my own mind.

I didn't. But that's what she said.

He sent her balloons on her birthday.

I met someone else.

And someone else.

I cut my wrist on a date's Rolex.

He thought this was a metaphor.

I thought he was a narcissist.

My ex dated my flatmate.

I asked her not to see him

but she said it was none of my business.

He started coming over.

I hated being at home.

My neighbour was a nudist

and washed his car in a thong.

My ex smoked roll-ups and burnt a hole in my bath

so I threw him out.

My landlord saw the bath and threw me out.

I moved far away.

I had a house party and tried to sleep with my
  cousin.
I took a trip to Cannes and was offered cash
to sleep with a race car driver.
I pretended I was flattered.
But that only made it worse.
He tried to bash down my hotel door.
I booked a flight I couldn't afford to get away.
My ex told my mum about my cousin.
My cousin told my mum about Cannes.
I bought Prada shoes and a vintage sewing box.
My cousin got married and I cried.
My ex got a distinction and I was jealous.
My mum sold the car in the garage for parts.
I met someone.
My ex bought a flat.
My ex never called me back.
I met someone.
I never called him back.

My cousin's kid is a famous DJ.

My neighbours' wisteria blooms along the fence.

I no longer pretend.

I hate cigarettes.

I love fast food.

I picked him up from the airport

and twenty minutes later,

in a Homebase car park,

we were laughing.


My mum's garage is empty.

I have included this poem, not because it is particularly joyful or uplifting, but because it states a wonderful truth: we all want to know what the future has in store for us, but the point is not where we end up but the very fact that we grow as we make our way there.

# In the Land of Giants

*George Szirtes*

Once everything was big
and you were small,
but year after year your shadow
crept up the wall
and you grew tall.

Quite frightening really
to think of that small shadow disappearing,
to hear that small voice passing out of hearing.

That's the trouble with growing:
you'd like to know where you are going,
but there's no knowing.

Edwin Morgan was the first ever Scottish national poet, known as The Scots Makar, and lived to the ripe old age of ninety.

# The Release

*Edwin Morgan*

The scaffolding has gone.* The sky is there! hard cold high clear
and blue.
Clanking poles and thudding planks were the music of a
strip-down that let light through
At last, hammered the cage door off its hinges, banged its
goodbye to the bantering dusty brickie crew,
Left us this rosy cliff-face telling the tentative sun it is almost as
good as new.
So now that we are so scoured and open and clean, what shall
we do?
There is so much to say
And who can delay
When some are lost and some are seen, our dearest heads, and
to those and to these we must still answer and be true.

* I really like this opening image. Anyone who has lived with scaffolding will know
what a liberating feeling it is when it's removed, and light pours in once again.

There is something about a new year, whether it's the calendar, academic or tax* year, that gives us pause. On the other side of that full stop is anything we choose.

* OK, maybe not the tax year!

# Poem for a New Year

*Matt Goodfellow*

Something's moving in,
I hear the weather in the wind,
sense the tension of a sheep-field
and the pilgrimage of fins.

Something's not the same,
I taste the sap and feel the grain,
hear the rolling of the rowan
ringing, singing in a change.

Something's set to start,
there's meadow-music in the dark
and the clouds that shroud the mountain
slowly, softly start to part.

Do you know this rhyme by heart? I think I came across it when I was four or five years old, but reading it now I see it's simply a non-religious prayer for better things to come. How many of us have looked into the night sky and wished upon a star? 'I wish, I wish, I wish ...' The stars always make me feel so small, yet weirdly magical and powerful.

# Star Light, Star Bright

*Anon.*

Star light, star bright,
First star I see tonight,
I wish I may, I wish I might,
Have this wish I wish tonight.

Many years ago I was on a flight from New York to Puerto Rico, when the pilot warned us that we were about to enter some severe turbulence. He told us to put on our seatbelts and remain calm. And I was calm. Calm, that is, until the turbulence actually began. I have experienced nothing like it before and nothing like it since. The plane buckled and intermittently nosedived for approximately twenty minutes and for the first time in years, I started to pray. Of course, everything was OK. We landed. And the next day I took another flight. But those moments in the air, when I wasn't sure whether or not I'd make it to Puerto Rico alive, made me oh so grateful for all the gifts around me.

# The Earth Shakes

*Steve Sanfield*

The earth shakes
just enough
to remind us.

Dickinson published only ten poems during her lifetime, but wrote close to 1,800, and is now considered to be a leading figure in American poetry.

In '"Hope" is the thing with feathers', Dickinson portrays hope as a bird that lives within the human spirit and 'never stops'.

# 'Hope' is the thing with feathers

*Emily Dickinson*

'Hope' is the thing with feathers –
That perches in the soul –
And sings the tune without the words –
And never stops – at all –

And sweetest – in the Gale – is heard –
And sore must be the storm –
That could abash the little Bird
That kept so many warm –

I've heard it in the chillest land –
And on the strangest Sea –
Yet – never – in Extremity,
It asked a crumb – of Me.

# Promise

*Jackie Kay*

Remember, the time of year
when the future appears
like a blank sheet of paper
a clean calendar, a new chance.
On thick white snow

You vow fresh footprints
then watch them go
with the wind's hearty gust.
Fill your glass. Here's tae us. Promises
made to be broken, made to last.*

* It is a delight to make resolutions, but OK to break them!

I first came across Brecht at university, where I studied his very well-known play, *Mother Courage and Her Children*. This short, beautiful poem, however, is the piece of work by him I most love.

# When the times darken

*Bertolt Brecht*

In the dark times
Will there be singing?
There will be singing.
Of the dark times.

This is the last poem in a novel of mine called *Moonrise*. It's about a teenager called Joe, who must say goodbye to his brother Ed, who is on death row. It's a book about family and love and justice. This final poem is a bit of a spoiler, I'm afraid; it is about how to find hope when all seems lost.

# from **Moonrise**

# **Back in Arlington**

*Sarah Crossan*

The sky is bright blue,
the pavements peppered with old bits of gum and
cracked from years of carrying people.

I go into our house,
my bedroom,
the place I used to share with Ed.

My bed is made,
but the blinds are shut
making it seem like night-time.

Something glitters
on the bookcase.
I follow the glint.

It's a plastic, glow-in-the-dark
crescent moon
no wider than a dime.

I hold it in the palm of my hand.
The arc smiles up at me.

I didn't know I had this in here.
It must have been Ed's from years ago.

I fold my fingers around the plastic piece
and scan the room for other signs of moons or stars,
Ed
hidden in the everyday,
burrowed away in my life forever.

Because you never know
what you might find in the dark.

The repetition of the phrase 'shake my future' actually makes me feel like I am being given a good shake!

# Shake My Future

*Dorothea Smartt*

shake my future push me past my complacency
my taken-for-granted my comfort zone
shake my future let me source the unimagined
be released from the sentence of the inevitable
take control, empower myself
past the dour predictions of the present
and change myself
shake my future challenge our 'first world's
capitalist consumerist criminal zone
of perpetual purchasing
shake my future past the edges of the known
world launch me out into the hinterlands
of the intuited imagined
beyond the droughts of apathy
and quench my thirst for something different
shake my future with alternative endings
curdle the milk of human kindness beyond
the patronising rattle of charity cans
to preserve the poor and assuage my guilt
shake my future with a kaleidoscope of tunes

play some other melody and bliss me out
of ignorance let my mind expand with a question
and seeking the answers shake my future
shake my future shake my future
in a triangle of tangential tirades and beckon me
into a sandwich of yes we can and hope

'Waiting' is one of the poems I am most excited to introduce you to, as it's written by an incredibly talented young poet, only eighteen years old at the time of going to print. I came across Joshua Cullen's work during my term as the Laureate na nÓg (Ireland's Children's Literature Laureate), when I spearheaded the project called We Are The Poets. The aim of the project was to encourage teenagers to see themselves as poets by reminding them that language belongs to all of us. Cullen emerged as a particular talent and continues to write.

# Waiting

*Joshua Cullen*

From treasured times of being young
To making plans throughout the year,
Back then, as soon as the day was done,
Tomorrow had always seemed so clear.

And so the year had come to pass
When life had changed for you and me,
We thought these times would never last,
But now that's just a distant dream

The achievements you made, they took you somewhere,
From the very same path that takes you back home,
But now if you feel that this path leads you nowhere,
Just know that you're not the only one.

To find the light in the darkest days,
Your friends were there to give you the strength,
But now if you feel that you've drifted away,
Just know that, someday, you'll meet them again.

I know that it's easy for me to say,

And I cannot speak for everyone,

But although that these times are here to stay,

There will be better things to come.


For now, I'll watch the sun descend

Until I drift away, and dream

Of better times towards the end,

In which we hope to finally reach.

It feels important to note that in 1939, at fifteen years of age, Mueller and her family fled Nazi Germany and settled in the United States.

# Hope

*Lisel Mueller*

It hovers in dark corners
before the lights are turned on,
    it shakes sleep from its eyes
    and drops from mushroom gills,
        it explodes in the starry heads
        of dandelions turned sages,
            it sticks to the wings of green angels
            that sail from the tops of maples.

It sprouts in each occluded eye
of the many-eyed potato,
    it lives in each earthworm segment
    surviving cruelty,
        it is the motion that runs
        from the eyes to the tail of a dog,
            it is the mouth that inflates the lungs
            of the child that has just been born.

It is the singular gift
we cannot destroy in ourselves,*
the argument that refutes death,
the genius that invents the future,
all we know of God.

It is the serum which makes us swear
not to betray one another;
it is in this poem, trying to speak.

* To be honest, I sometimes wish I *could* destroy hope – because
  it makes me long for things that can never be.

Being in the 'belly of the whale' means to be in a period of intense soul searching, when you let go of the past and enter a new stage of life. It is part of what is called the 'hero's journey', and takes its name from the biblical story of Jonah and the Whale.

# Things to Do in the Belly of the Whale

*Dan Albergotti*

Measure the walls. Count the ribs. Notch the long days.
Look up for blue sky through the spout. Make small fires
with the broken hulls of fishing boats. Practice smoke signals.
Call old friends, and listen for echoes of distant voices.
Organize your calendar. Dream of the beach. Look each way
for the dim glow of light. Work on your reports.\* Review
each of your life's ten million choices. Endure moments
of self-loathing.† Find the evidence of those before you.
Destroy it. Try to be very quiet, and listen for the sound
of gears and moving water. Listen for the sound of your heart.♥
Be thankful that you are here, swallowed with all hope,
where you can rest and wait. Be nostalgic. Think of all
the things you did and could have done. Remember
treading water in the center of the still night sea, your toes
pointing again and again down, down into the black depths.

\* Whilst we turn from a caterpillar into a butterfly, it is reasonable to keep
  up with admin!
† I am pleased to find I am normal, and that self-loathing is simply a part
  of the soul-searching process!
♥ 'Yes!'

Anne Sexton began writing poetry as a sort of therapy for severe depression after she suffered a breakdown and her doctor suggested she write about her feelings. Her work is sometimes described as 'confessional' as it is so deeply personal. Despite Sexton's ongoing mental health issues, she won many awards for her work during her lifetime. Sadly, Sexton took her own life when she was forty-six years of age.

I include this poem for anyone battling depression.

# Welcome Morning

*Anne Sexton*

There is joy
in all:
in the hair I brush each morning,
in the Cannon towel, newly washed,
that I rub my body with each morning,
in the chapel of eggs I cook
each morning,
in the outcry from the kettle
that heats my coffee
each morning,
in the spoon and the chair
that cry 'hello there, Anne'
each morning,
in the godhead of the table
that I set my silver, plate, cup upon
each morning.

All this is God,
right here in my pea-green house
each morning
and I mean,
though often forget,
to give thanks,
to faint down by the kitchen table
in a prayer of rejoicing
as the holy birds at the kitchen window
peck into their marriage of seeds.

So while I think of it,
let me paint a thank-you on my palm
for this God, this laughter of the morning,
lest it go unspoken.

The Joy that isn't shared, I've heard,
dies young.

The next three poems feature rain. In the first, by Teasdale, the rain feels positive, softly bringing with it the joy of spring. In the second, by Longfellow, rainy weather is an unfortunate part of the ritual of the seasons – you can't have summer without winter. I like both of these very much, not because I'm devoted to nature, but because I like the idea of the inevitability of spring and summer following the dark days of winter. OK, today isn't a picnic, but, you know, 'some days must be dark and dreary'.

The third rainy poem by Kaplinski is different again: the very possibility of rain brings hope. Rain produces spinach and dill, and if water alone can do this, what else can be created or achieved?

# There Will Come Soft Rains

*Sara Teasdale*

There will come soft rains and the smell of the ground,
And swallows calling with their shimmering sound;

And frogs in the pools singing at night,
And wild-plum trees in tremulous white;

Robins will wear their feathery fire,
Whistling their whims on a low fence-wire;

And not one will know of the war, not one
Will care at last when it is done.

Not one would mind, neither bird nor tree,
if mankind perished utterly;

And Spring herself, when she woke at dawn,
Would scarcely know that we were gone.

# The Rainy Day

*Henry Wadsworth Longfellow*

The day is cold, and dark, and dreary;
It rains, and the wind is never weary;
The vine still clings to the mouldering wall,
But at every gust the dead leaves fall,
    And the day is dark and dreary.

My life is cold, and dark, and dreary;
It rains, and the wind is never weary;
My thoughts still cling to the mouldering Past,
But the hopes of youth fall thick in the blast,
    And the days are dark and dreary.

Be still, sad heart! and cease repining;
Behind the clouds is the sun still shining;
Thy fate is the common fate of all,
Into each life some rain must fall,
    Some days must be dark and dreary.

# The Possibility of Rain ...

*Jaan Kaplinski*

The possibility of rain ... If rain is possible
everything is possible: spinach, lettuce, radish and dill,
even carrots and potatoes, even black
and red currants, even swallows
above the pond where you can see
the reflection of the full moon, and bats flying.
The children finish playing badminton and go in.
There's a haze to the west. Little by little
the fatigue in my limbs changes to optimism.* I dream
I borrow a plane to fly to Cologne.
I must go in too. The sky's nearly dark,
a half-moon shining through birch branches.
Suddenly I feel myself like an alchemist's retort
where all this – heat, boredom,
hope and new thoughts –
is melting into something strange, colourful and new.

* 'Little by little', despair turns to hope. We needn't rush it. A day at a time.

I am not a religious person, but the lapsed Catholic becomes alert at these lines.

# from **Psalm 30**

For his anger lasts only a moment, but his favour lasts a lifetime;
weeping may stay for the night, but rejoicing comes in the morning.

Carruth wrote this poem in response to the pandemic.
I think the opening words could be the inspiration for
many more original works: 'For the times ahead / when ...'

# the long bench

*Jim Carruth*

For the times ahead
when we will be

as if at either end
of the long bench

where distance kept
is love's measure

and death dances
the space between

when words alone
are not enough

and queued memories
reach out to touch

let longing be a store
of nut and seed

that grows each day
in strange hibernation

readying for its end –
the sharing of the feast.

My friend Nikki and I have a sort of ongoing joke that
when times are hard (when *aren't* they hard?), we
text one another messages such as 'hope you have
a satisfactory day' or 'if you are alive, you did well'.
I think of Mahon's poem in the same way I think of
those messages – as an acknowledgement that times
are tough but that ultimately 'the sun rises in spite of
everything', and if it does, everything might be all right.

# Everything Is Going to Be All Right

*Derek Mahon*

How should I not be glad to contemplate
the clouds clearing beyond the dormer window
and a high tide reflected on the ceiling?
There will be dying, there will be dying,
but there is no need to go into that.
The lines flow from the hand unbidden
and the hidden source is the watchful heart;
the sun rises in spite of everything
and the far cities are beautiful and bright.
I lie here in a riot of sunlight
watching the day break and the clouds flying.
Everything is going to be all right.

When I read this excerpt from *The Cure at Troy*, I cannot help but imagine President Joe Biden. That is because this is one of Biden's favourite poems, and if you take a look at President Biden's YouTube channel, you'll be able to hear Biden himself reading it aloud.

If you want to read more by Seamus Heaney, which I would recommend, you could follow this with 'Blackberry-Picking' or 'Digging', two of his most popular poems.

# from **The Cure at Troy**

*Seamus Heaney*

Human beings suffer.
They torture one another.
They get hurt and get hard.
No poem or play or song
Can fully right a wrong
Inflicted and endured.

History says, Don't hope
On this side of the grave,
But then, once in a lifetime
The longed-for tidal wave
Of justice can rise up
And hope and history rhyme.

So hope for a great sea-change
On the far side of revenge.
Believe that the farther shore
Is reachable from here.
Believe in miracles
And cures and healing wells.

Call miracle self-healing,

The utter self-revealing

Double-take of feeling.

If there's fire on the mountain

And lightning and storm

And a god speaks from the sky

That means someone is hearing

The outcry and birth-cry

Or new life at its term.

It means once in a lifetime

That justice can rise up

And hope and history rhyme.

I hope this one speaks for itself. It's for you, if you've been sad. I know how that feels. And I know it gets better. Sending you so much love. Sarah xx

# tomorrow is beautiful

*Sarah Crossan*

beyond the wall of now,
tomorrow is waiting.

its light is longing to find you;

      look for its glow
      in the corner you had forgotten.

beyond the cold brick of today
tomorrow knows better.

it is waffles and blackberries,
tea and buttered cake,
it is a robin on your windowsill,
his puffed red belly striving for song.

beyond the hard silence of here,
tomorrow is beckoning.

it is an unexpected love letter.
it is a long kiss.

it is not crying,
not *always* crying.

because
tomorrow is beautiful.

tomorrow is beautiful.

# Thanks

Thank you to the poets included in this anthology for giving us permission to include your work in our book. I feel so humbled to sit alongside you.

Without the dedication of Zöe Griffiths, my editor, this anthology would never have come together as wonderfully as it has. So thank you, as always, for being amazing, Zöe! Thank you also to Beth Dufour, Jadene Squires, Fliss Stevens, Beatrice Cross, Jade Westwood, Jet Purdie, Jeni Child, Michael Young and the whole Bloomsbury Children's team.

Thank you to my agent, Julia Churchill, who has put up with me for ten years now. You are the very best. (And I'm your favourite, right?)

Many friends pointed me in the direction of poems they love which may or may not have made it into this book, but I was grateful for the ideas. Thank you especially to Charlotte Hacking, Aingeala Flannery, Nikki Sheehan, Phil Earle and Erin Whitcraft.

Thank you also to the vast number of poets, academics and organisations for creating resources I was able to draw from to help compile this book, including Pádraig Ó Tuama, Jeanette Winterson, Jack Underwood, Rachael Allen, National Poetry Day, Poetry Ireland, The Poetry Society, Scottish Poetry Library, CLPE, Poetry Foundation and Poetry By Heart.

Thank you finally to Aoife. I love you more than anything: you are my beautiful tomorrow.

# Index of First Lines

# Index of Poets

# Acknowledgements

The compiler and publisher would like to thank the following for permission to use copyright material:

*From* Psalm 30, taken from the Holy Bible, New International Version®, NIV®. Copyright © 1973, 1978, 1984, 2011 by Biblica, Inc.™ Used by permission of Zondervan. All rights reserved worldwide. www.zondervan.com The 'NIV' and 'New International Version' are trademarks registered in the United States Patent and Trademark Office by Biblica, Inc.®; **Ahmed, Dilruba**, 'PHASE ONE' from *Bring Now the Angels* by Dilruba Ahmed © 2020. Reprinted by permission of the University of Pittsburgh Press; **Albergotti, Dan**, 'Things to Do in the Belly of the Whale' from *The Boatloads*, BOA Editions Ltd, 2008. Reproduced with permission from D. Albergotti; **Alexander, Kwame**, 'Majestic' © Kwame Alexander 2021. Reproduced with permission; **Anaxagorou, Anthony**, 'It Will Come to You' and 'For All You've Endured', edited by the author for this edition in 2021, from the original versions of these works, found in *Heterogeneous*, published by Out-Spoken Press in 2016. Reproduced by permission of Greene & Heaton Ltd; **Angelou, Maya**, 'Still I Rise' from *And Still I Rise: A Book of Poems*, Random House, 1978. Reproduced with permission; **Brecht, Bertolt**, 'When the times darken' originally published in German in 1939 as 'Motto: In den finsteren Zeiten', translated by Tom Kuhn. Copyright © 1976, 1961 by Bertolt-Brecht-Erben/Suhrkamp Verlag, from *Collected Poems of Bertolt Brecht* by Bertolt Brecht, translated by Tom Kuhn and David Constantine. Used by permission of Liveright Publishing Corporation; **Bulley, Victoria Adukwei**, 'Love' from *Rising Stars – New Voices in Poetry*, Otter Barry Books, 2017, p.39. Reproduced with permission from Otter Barry Books; **Carruth, Jim**, 'the long bench' © Jim Carruth 2020; **Constantine, David**, 'The Wasps', from *David Constantine – Collected Poems* (Bloodaxe Books, 2004). Reproduced with permission from Bloodaxe Books; **Cook, Abigail**, 'Rise' from *Rising Stars – New Voices in Poetry*, Otter Barry Books, 2017, p.50. Reproduced with permission from Otter Barry Books; **Cookson, Paul**, 'Let No One Steal Your Dreams' © Paul Cookson 2021. Reproduced with permission; **Crossan, Sarah**, 'until', 'More in the Moment', 'Notes from the Pit', 'Why Bother, Mother?', 'These I Have Loved', '*from* Here is the Beehive', 'Rise', 'you are enough', 'Things You Put Into Your Mother's Garage And Try To Forget', 'Back in Arlington' (from *Moonrise*) and 'tomorrow is beautiful' reproduced by permission of the author; **Cullen, Joshua**, 'Waiting' © Joshua Cullen 2021.

# About Sarah Crossan

SARAH CROSSAN has lived in Dublin, London
and New York, and now lives in East Sussex.
She graduated with a degree in philosophy and
literature before training as an English and drama
teacher at the University of Cambridge.

The author of five multi-award-winning novels for
teenagers, including her heart-wrenching, bestselling
novel *One*, Sarah published her first book for adults,
*Here Is the Beehive*, in 2020 to great critical acclaim.
She was the Laureate na nÓg (Ireland's Children's
Literature Laureate) from 2018 to 2020.

@SarahCrossan
@sarahcrossanwriter

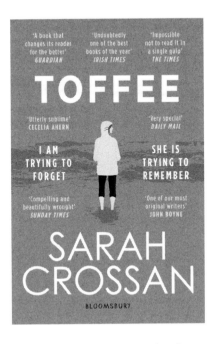

'A book that changes its reader for the better'
GUARDIAN

'Undoubtedly one of the best books of the year'
IRISH TIMES

'Impossible not to read it in a single gulp'
THE TIMES

# TOFFEE

'Utterly sublime'
CECELIA AHERN

'Very special'
DAILY MAIL

I AM TRYING TO FORGET

SHE IS TRYING TO REMEMBER

'Compelling and beautifully wrought'
SUNDAY TIMES

'One of our most original writers'
JOHN BOYNE

## SARAH CROSSAN

BLOOMSBURY

When Allison runs away from home she doesn't expect to be taken in by Marla, an elderly woman with dementia, who mistakes her for an old friend called Toffee. Allison is used to hiding who she really is and trying to be what other people want her to be. And so Toffee is who she becomes. But as her bond with Marla grows, Allison begins to ask herself – where is home? What is a family? And, most importantly, who am I really?

**'One of our most original writers'**
**John Boyne**

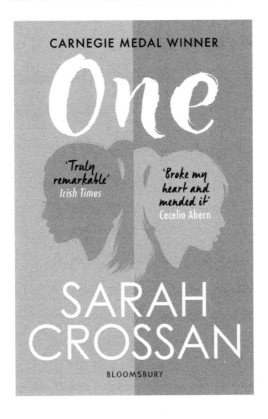

Grace and Tippi don't like being stared at, but they're used to it. They're conjoined twins – united in blood and bone. What they want is to be looked at like they truly are two people. They want real friends. And what about love?

**'Truly remarkable'**

*Irish Times*

Joe hasn't seen his brother for ten years, and it's for the most brutal of reasons. Ed is on death row. But now Ed's execution date has been set, and this might be the last summer they have together.

**'Impossible to put down ... Deep, light, witty and authentic'**
*The Times*

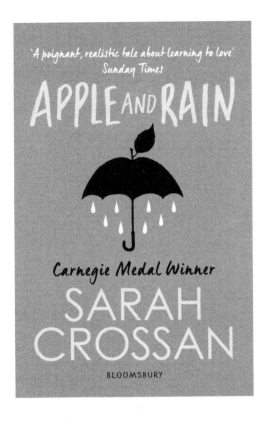

Apple's mother disappeared years ago, leaving Apple with her nana and a lot of unanswered questions. But when she unexpectedly explodes back into Apple's life like a comet, homecoming is bittersweet.

**'A poignant, realistic tale about learning to love ... and how poems can tell the truth'**
*Sunday Times*

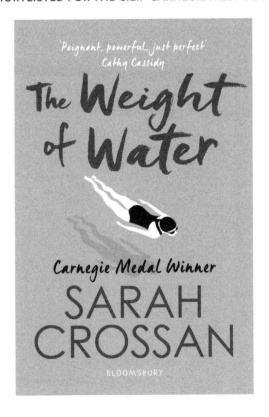

Life is lonely for Kasienka. She misses her old home
in Poland, her mother's heart is breaking, and at
her new English school friends are scarce. But when
someone new swims into her life, Kasienka learns
that there is more than one way to stay afloat.

**'Poignant, powerful, just perfect'**
**Cathy Cassidy**

*What would you do if you lost someone the world
never knew was yours?*

For three years, Ana has been consumed by an affair
with Connor. Their love has been consigned to hotel
rooms and dark corners of pubs, their relationship
kept hidden from the world. So the morning that
Ana receives a call to say that Connor is dead, her
secret grief has nowhere to go. Desperate for an
outlet, Ana seeks out the only person who might
understand – Connor's wife Rebecca ...

**'Unmissable ... Incredible'**
***Stylist***